AF478614

Places in the Sand

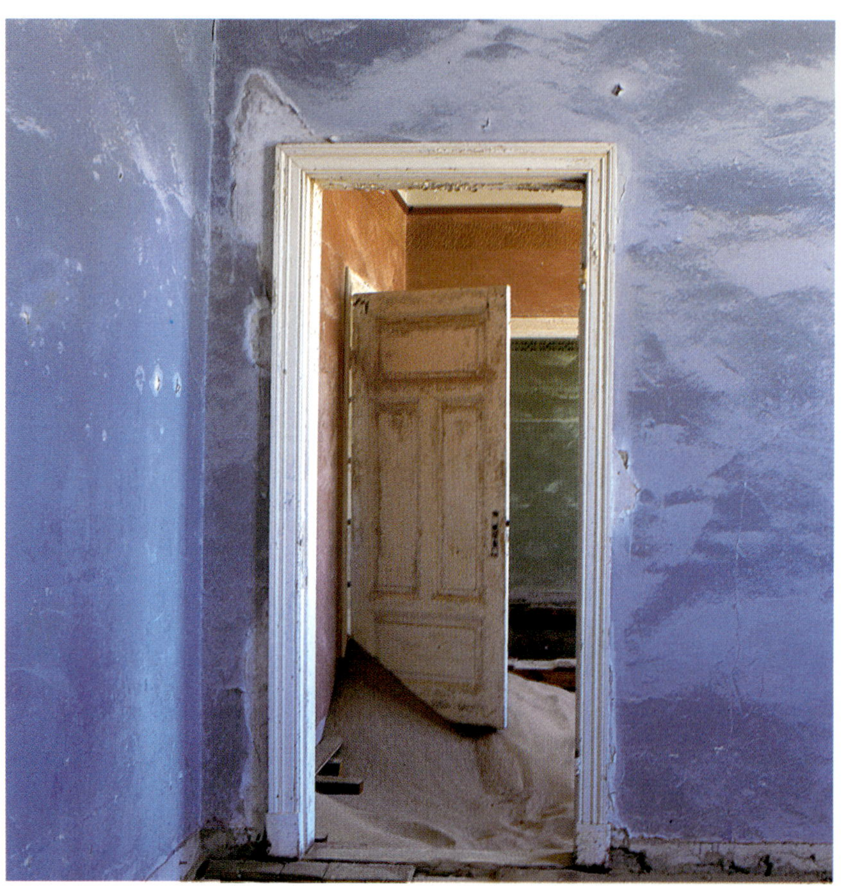

Journey through my place

Places in the Sand

Margaret Courtney-Clarke

THE MONACELLI PRESS

In memory of my father

The desert is the essence of nothing, and when I am among these mounds and mountains of sand the very reason for their being escapes me. God was distracted during the creation of these essential places that forged my character and my eye.

My photographs portray these places, my special places, places in the sand drenched with light and modeled by wind, where survival depends upon a drop of rain that may fall, or may not. In the sinuous dunes, my eye reads memories—memories less of place than of the emotions etched by desert places. The memories are from my childhood, but also from when I did not yet exist. And they are from when I shall no longer be, when the grains of sand will toil on, modifying the contours and the soft forms of the desert slowly, inevitably. These are not images that can be fixed in time or space; they are shards of my memory. For a moment a secret door in my mind opens to allow a glimpse of time-hazed recollections from a precious storehouse of remote treasures.

The desert is a place where I can listen to the emptiness of silence. It is the place where I was conceived and grew up, a revered place where I learned not to intrude upon the dignity of nature. It is an unspoiled land scarred by humankind. Nature heals, but only slowly and with pain.

With monotonous insistence, those scars, those traces impressed upon God's creation, persecute me. They are the roads that come from nowhere and into nowhere disappear again; the interminable fences marching across a vastness, erected to fight foot-and-mouth disease but cruelly subdividing the infinite and imprisoning the freedom of the land; the stirring signposts that read, with the presumption of humankind, "sand," "fish," or "no entry."

There is a silent village at the edge of a mine that had disgorged
quick riches, built as if overnight, only to be as swiftly reclaimed by
the elements after the last diamond was extracted. So too the house
in which I was born went back to the desert when my parents sur-
rendered to a ruthless drought. All these are but a few ephemeral
constructions of the White Man swallowed by the jaws of time.

Many years have passed. Lines are softened, contours and details
erased. What remains is veiled and indistinct save for a few details.
My thoughts soar to the endless horizons seared by sun and fogged
by mirages. Then they sink back again to nourish themselves on the
trembling of scorched air.

I recall our home, Liebig House, on the farm Neu-Heusis. Today it is an
eerie reminder of the grandeur of those years. Zebra and leopard
roamed the backyard and dignitaries from abroad were lavishly enter-
tained. Our daily outings entailed hunting partridge or kudu for the
pot or rowing in a dugout down at the gorge. Campfires in the open
veld and picnics under a camelthorn tree in a petrified riverbed con-
sisted of a three-legged iron cauldron and the wild smell of venison
carried by the wind. We children huddled by the fire to hear legends
about Bushman's Paradise—that lost oasis where children played with
diamonds—and the rock paintings of the White Lady and her hunters.
The stories were told by our adopted family, !N'gani and ≠Tommi,
members of the !Kung clan of the San people. We learned to distin-
guish the calls of birds and the gestures of animals and to draw suste-
nance from roots and melons. We learned to sharpen arrow points, to
extract poison from snakes, and to dig for water in a vast thirstland.
Above all, we learned to recognize the promise of rain. Everything I
needed to know in life I learned—or so it seemed then—from the San.

My memory leaps backward to those days when my father would
fly my mother, my sister, and me in our Piper Pacer toward the sea.
We thrilled at seeing the sunburnt plains of Tumas and Tinkas below

us as they unraveled beyond Moon Landscape all the way to the dunes of the Namib Desert. For a few hours we would soar over the arid desert toward the endless misty beach of the Skeleton Coast. From this unusual perspective we would spot herds of migrating game and, as much as a mile inland, sand-filled wrecks of ships, now the home of jackals. The voracious Namib took decades to swallow these stranded vessels into its sandy maw. We knew we had arrived once we caught a glimpse of the steel parallels of rail-road track that appeared just before our beach landing. There we would indulge in that greatest of joys for children of the desert, fishing in ice-cold waters and gathering bags of crayfish and mussels.

It was these images, in the shadow of our wings, that taught me to see the road I now travel. They opened a door for me.

I recall how time passed slowly through the train window on an eternal voyage that took four days to bring me home for school vacation. At times the boundless horizon was separated from the sky by a ribbon of pastel mountains. Sometimes these were indeed mountains, and sometimes merely reflections—a mirage. In such emptiness I lost a sense of proportion. Without points of reference miles seemed meters, until a single, tiny, dark impression, perhaps a tree or an ostrich or a small dik-dik, momentarily restored depth to the landscape.

Frequently we stopped under an implacable sun to scoop sand away from the scorching tracks. I remember the stops at isolated sidings to take on water and coal for the steam locomotive. I recall the thrill of seeing the wheels churn over the miles of track between sand dunes and ocean shore. And most of all I recall grains of sand rushing off with the wind, only to settle like pink flamingos in flight in some distant place to give birth to infant dunes.

Only memories have survived in the silence of the desert. All the rest of this is gone.

Memories of Neu-Heusis

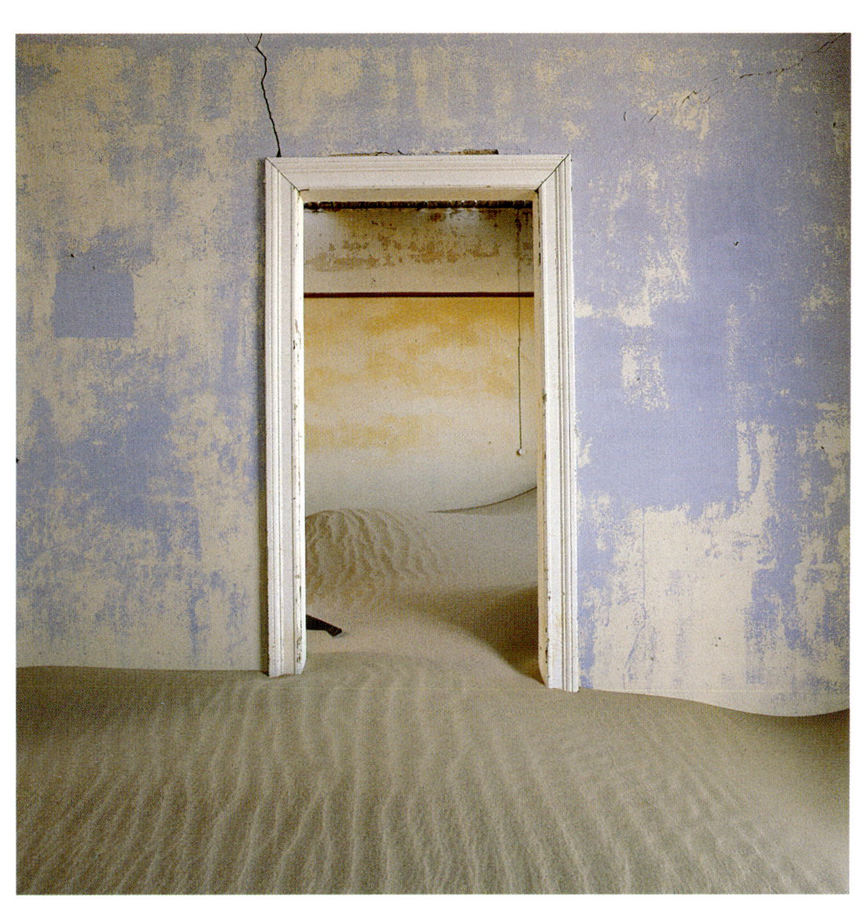

Mare Tranquillitatis

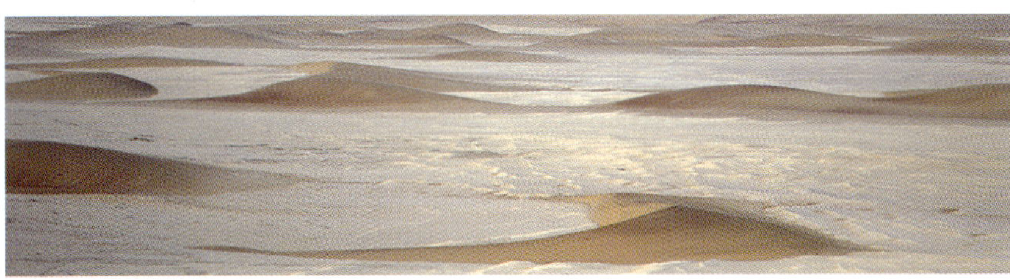

Sand in flight

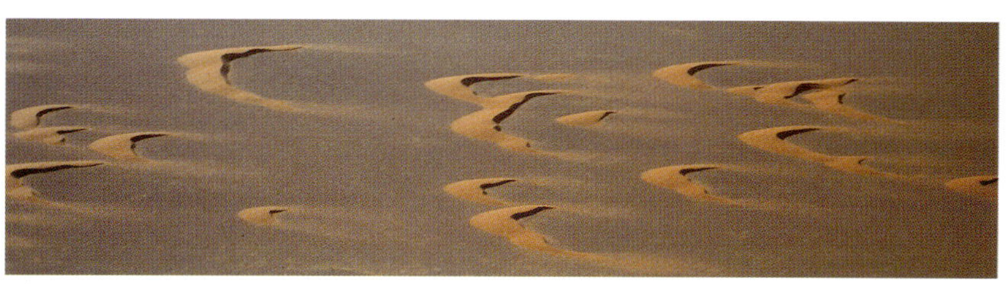

Earth's cradle #2

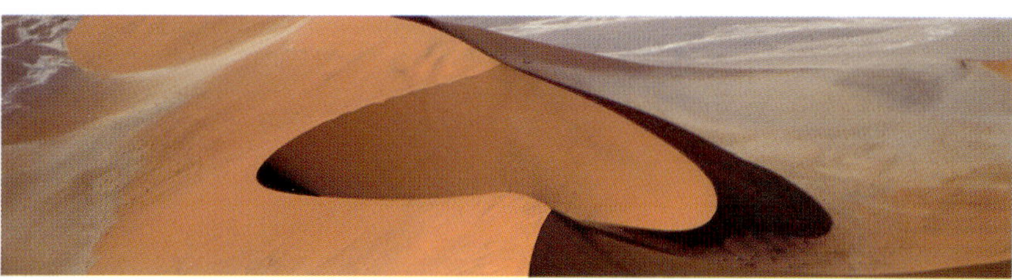

Star dune of the Namib

Waterless river

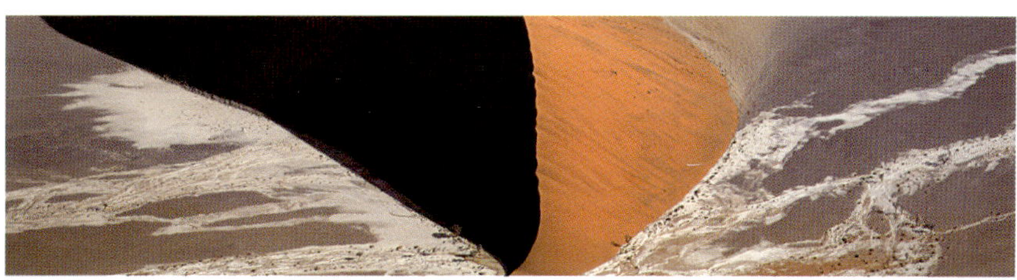

Five trees

Seven-year drought

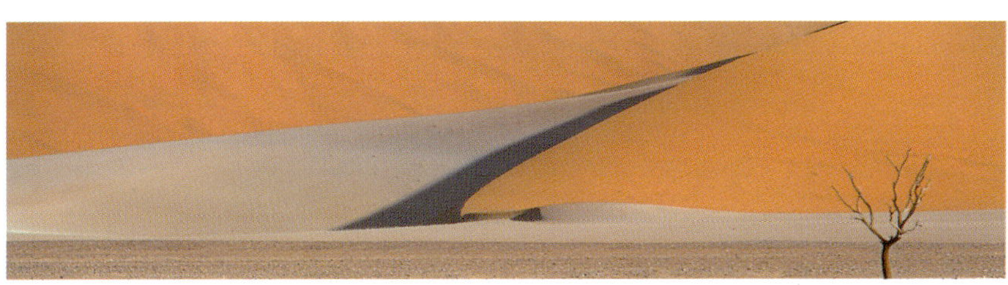

Thunderstorm on the plain

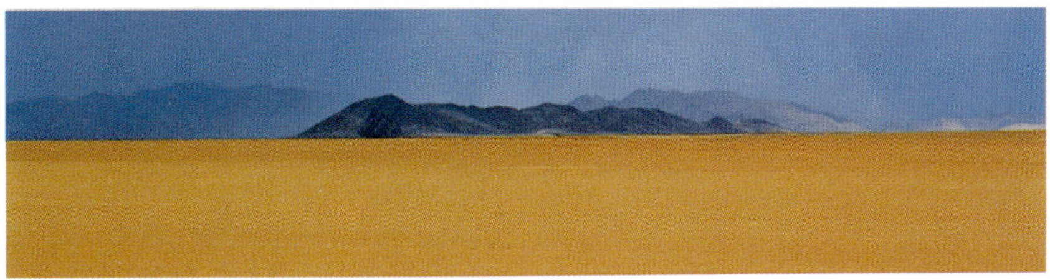

Leopard's canyon

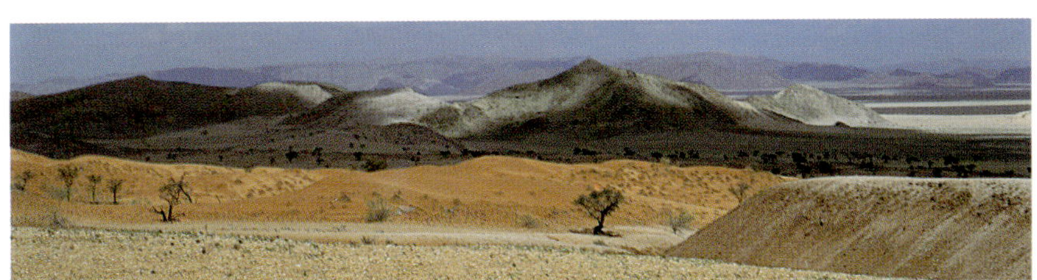

Dead tree #13

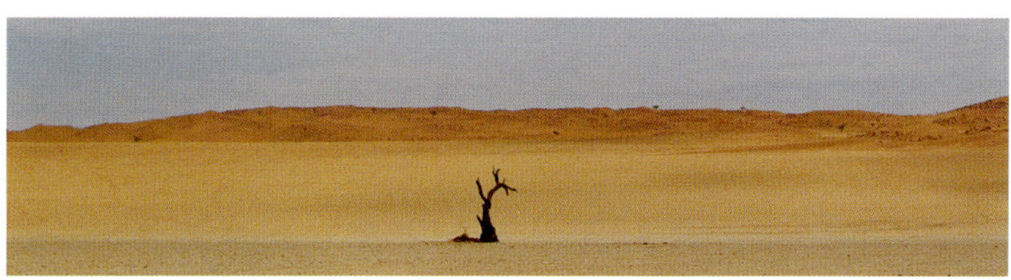

White Lady of Burnt Mountain

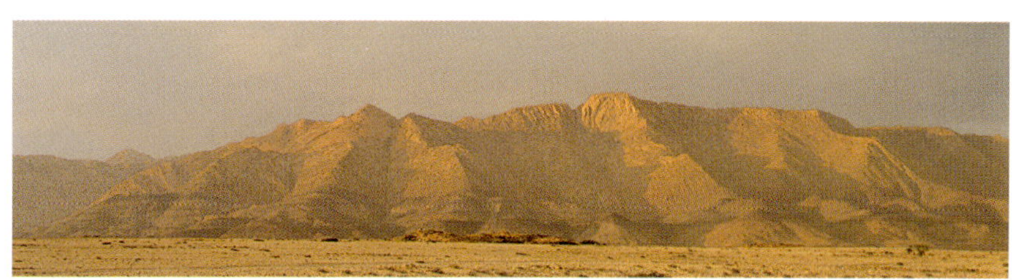

Singing dunes

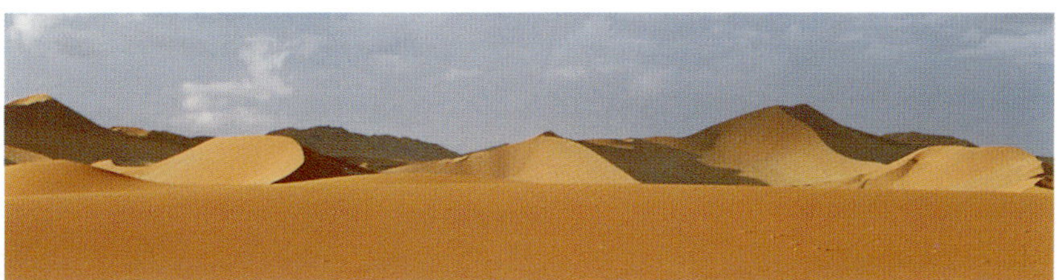

Deep sand

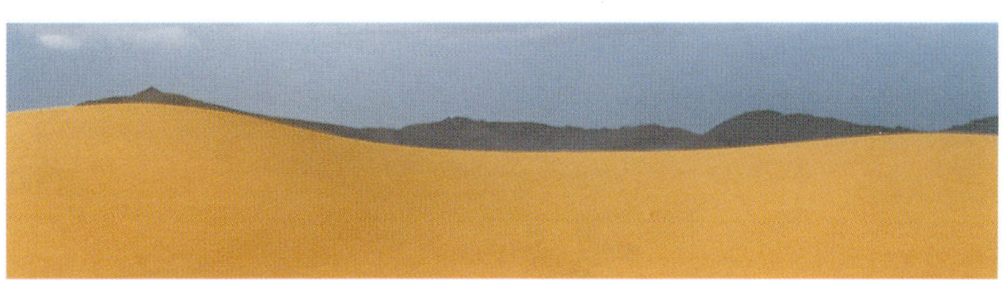

Rainbow

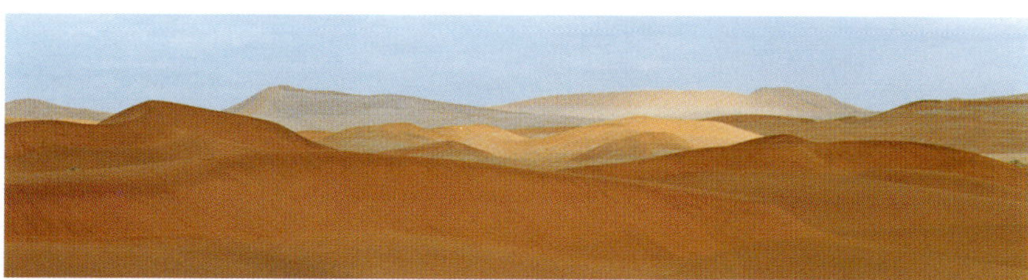

Unfolding dune

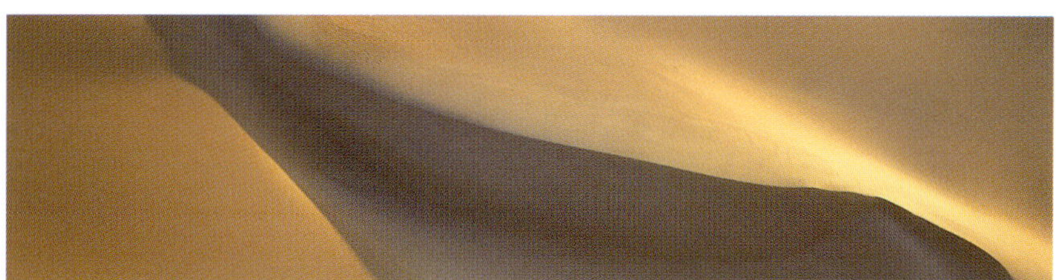

Shade in the east

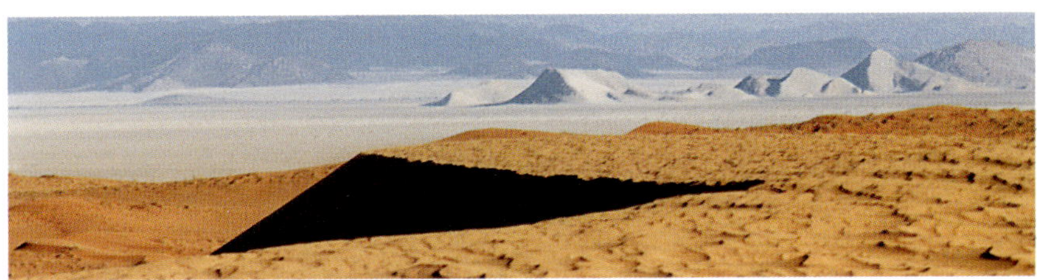

Curve of Dune 45

Cheops

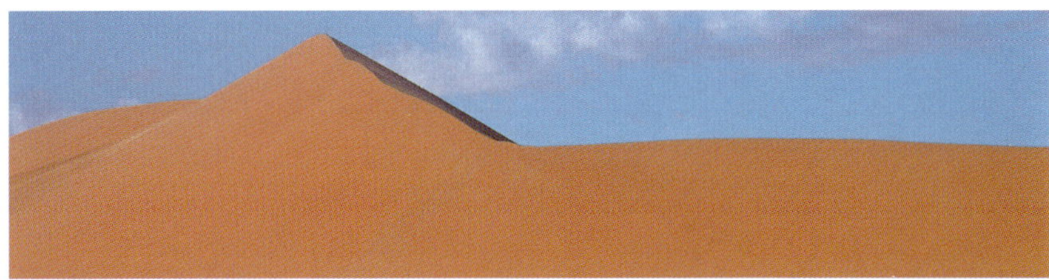

Thirstland

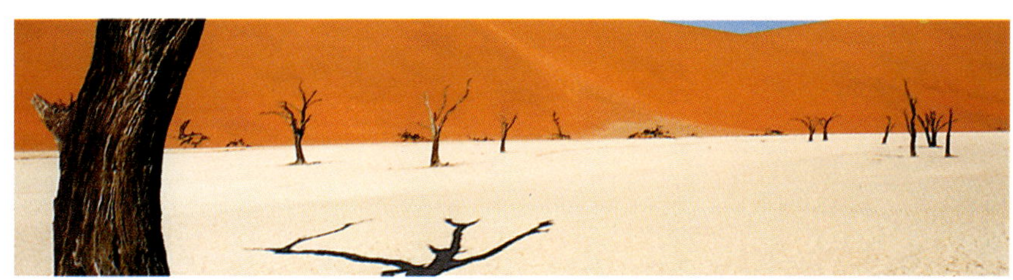

Crow's nest

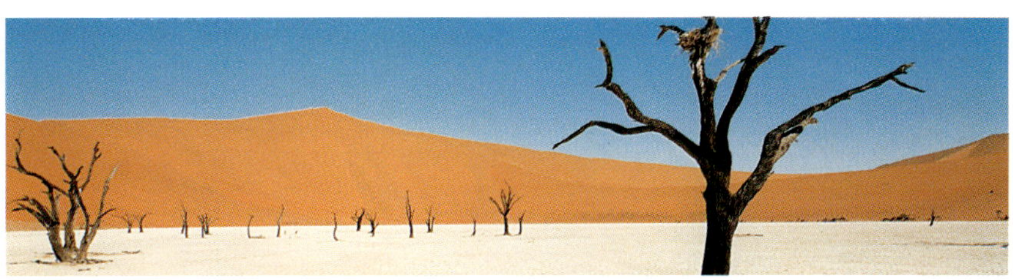

Underground river

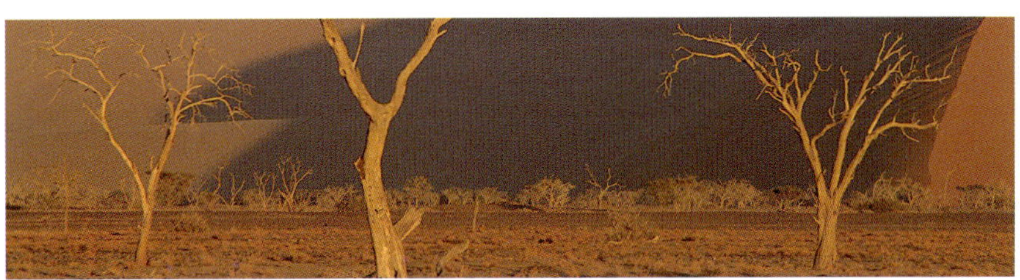

Midwife's residence

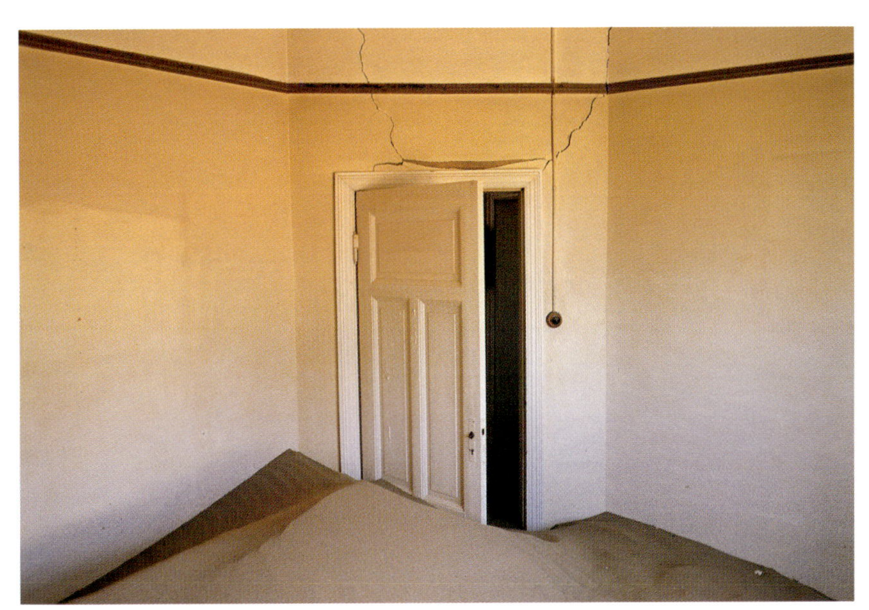

Long beach

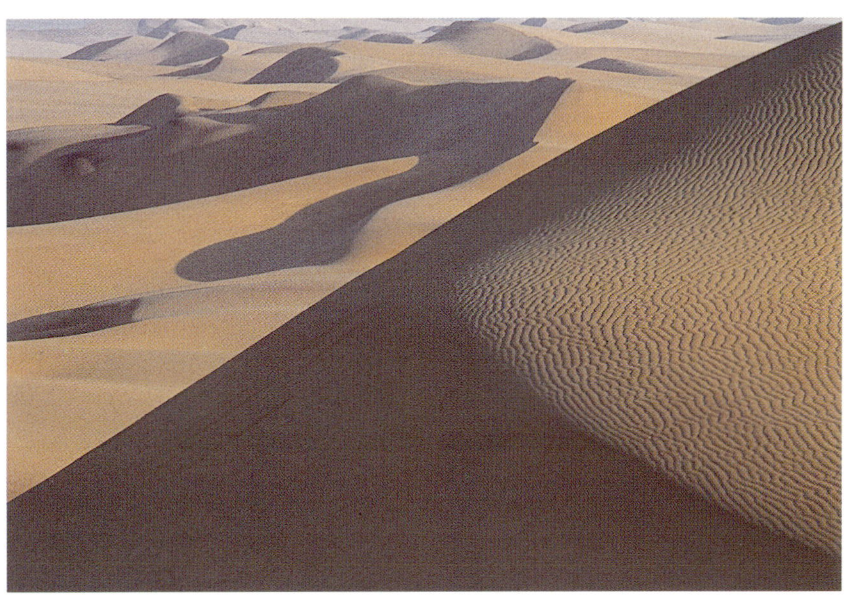

Three generations

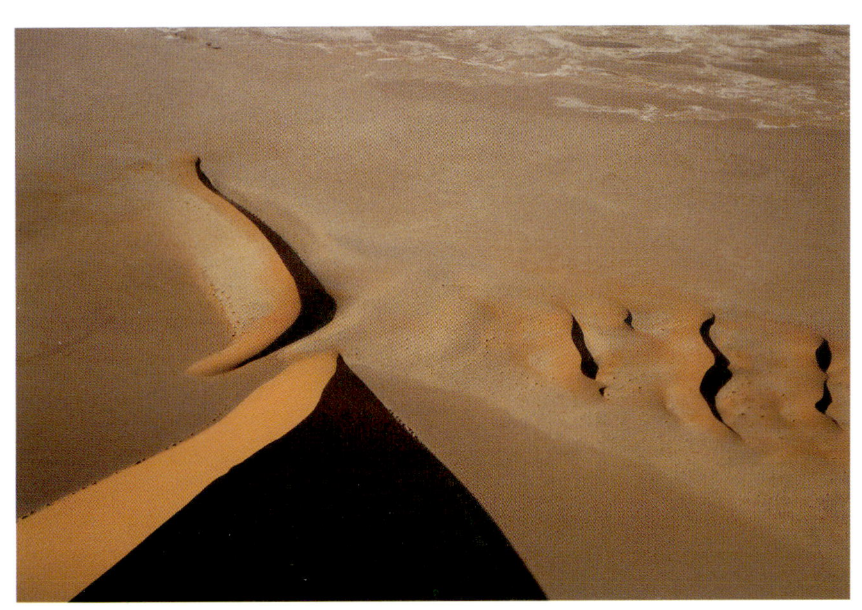

Going somewhere

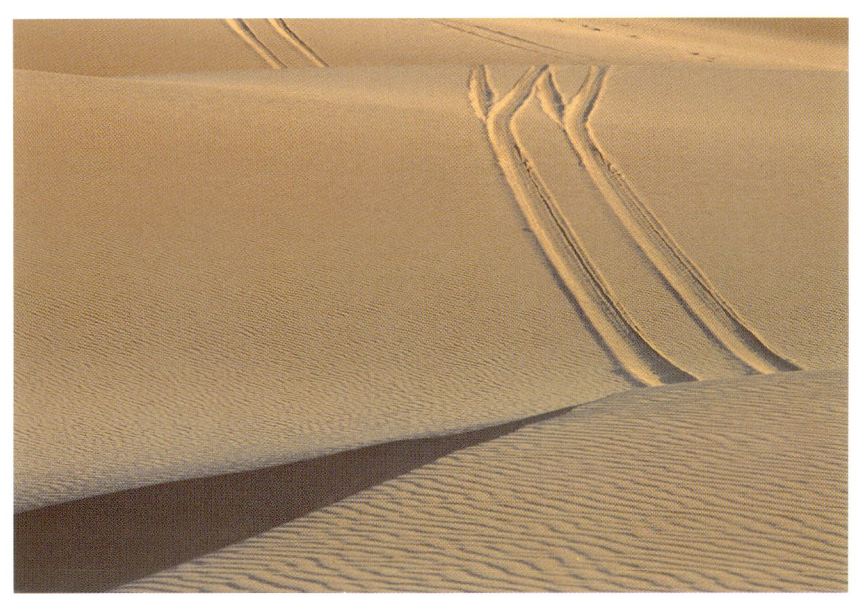

Struggle

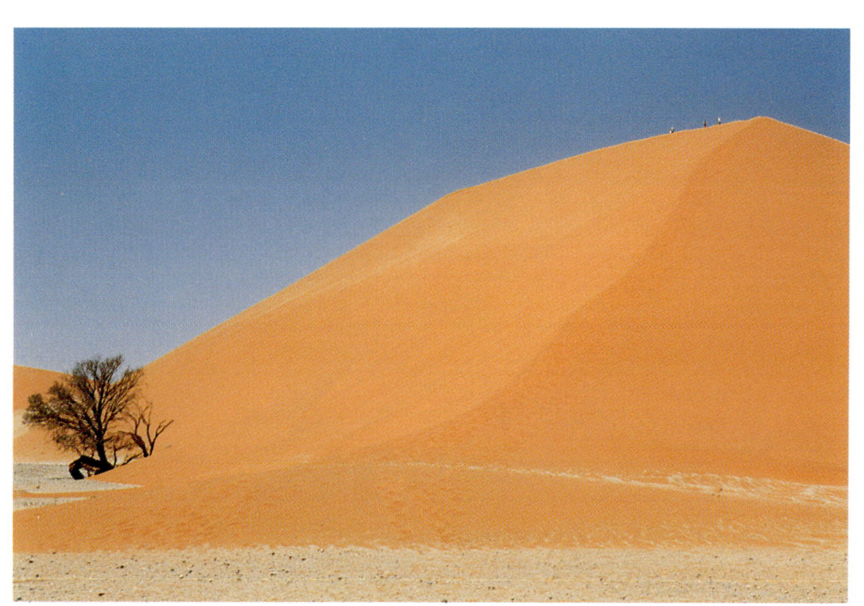

Blue sky

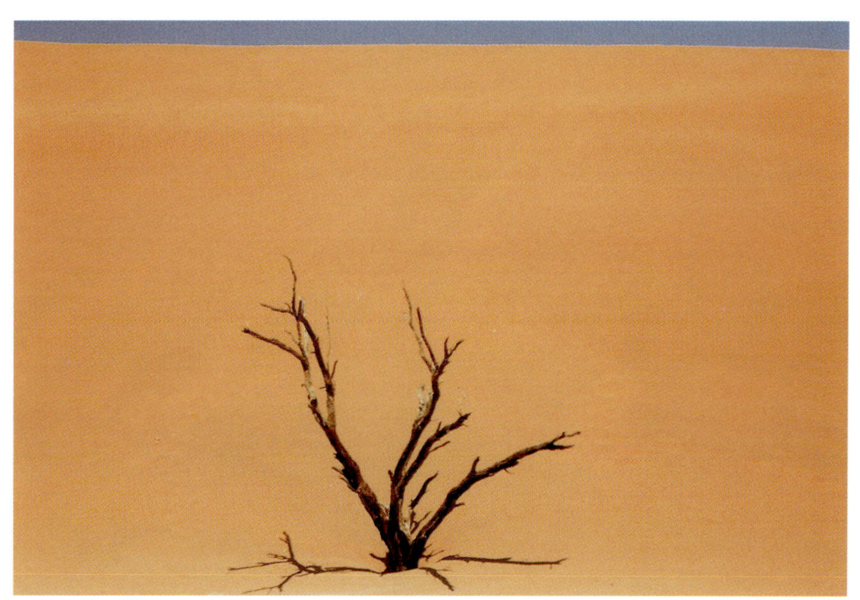

Shelter

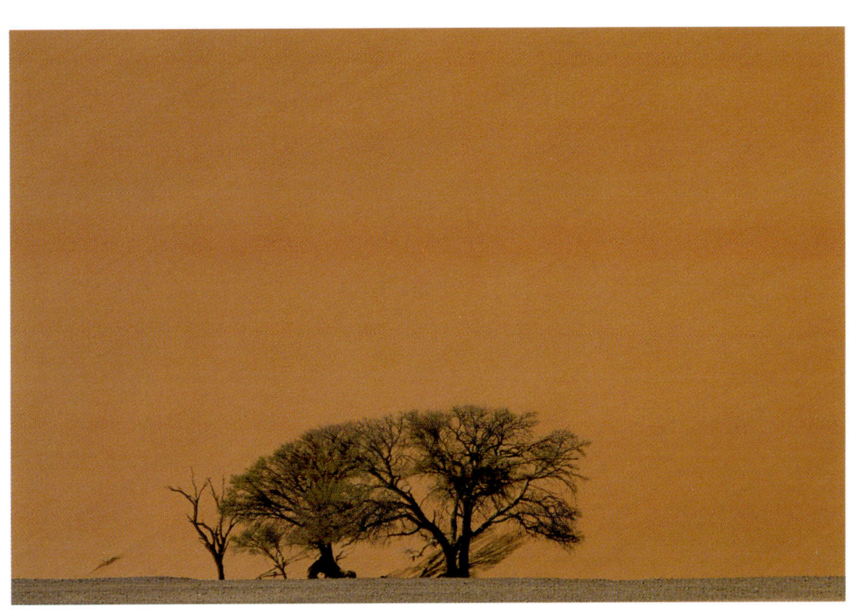

White Mountain

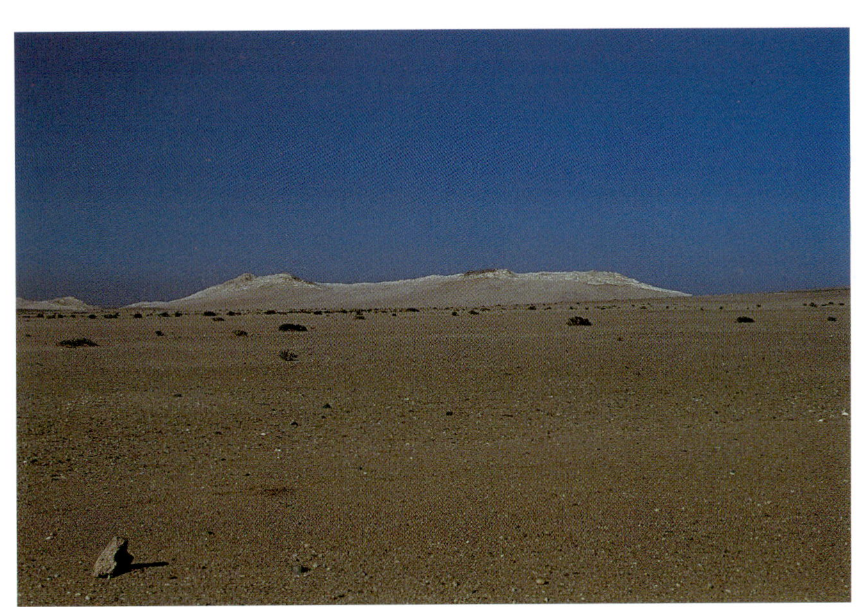

Mine manager's residence

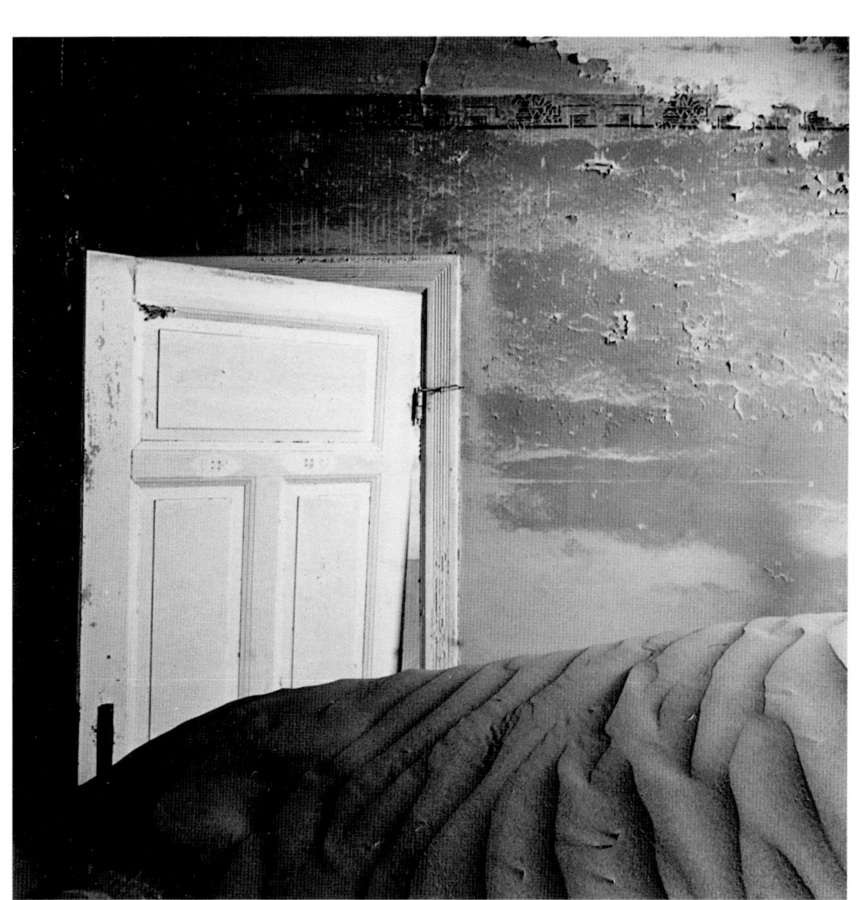

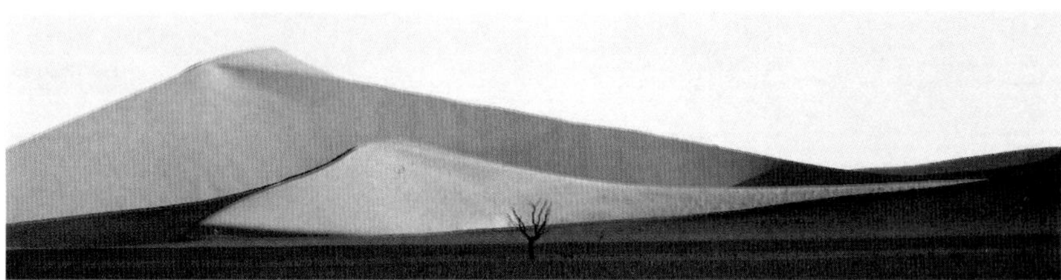

Wind, sand, and tree

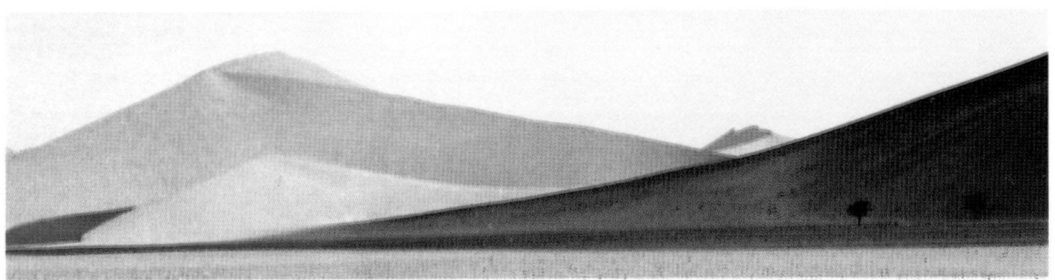

Wind, sand, and infinity

Silence in the sand

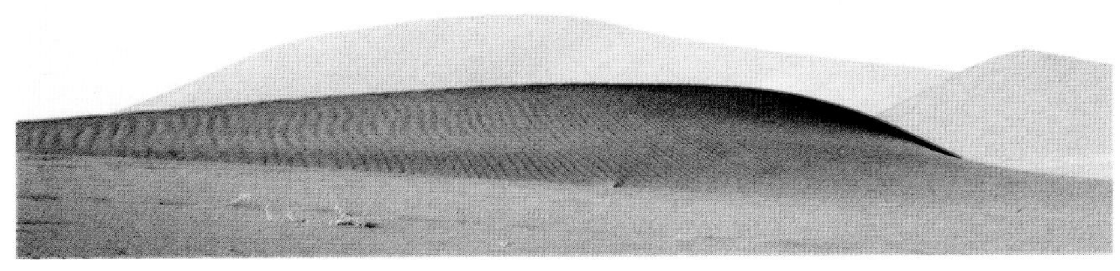

Riding out the wind

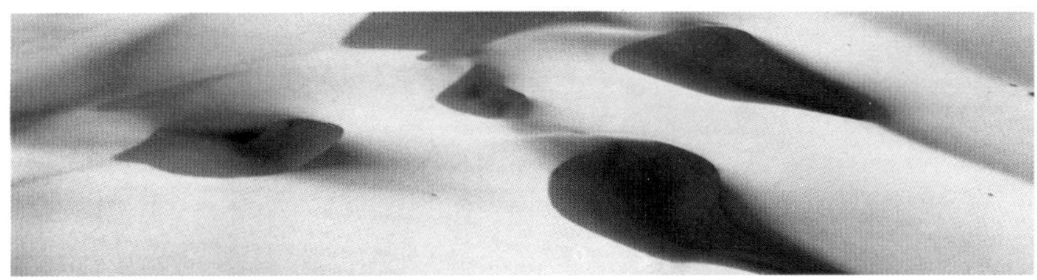

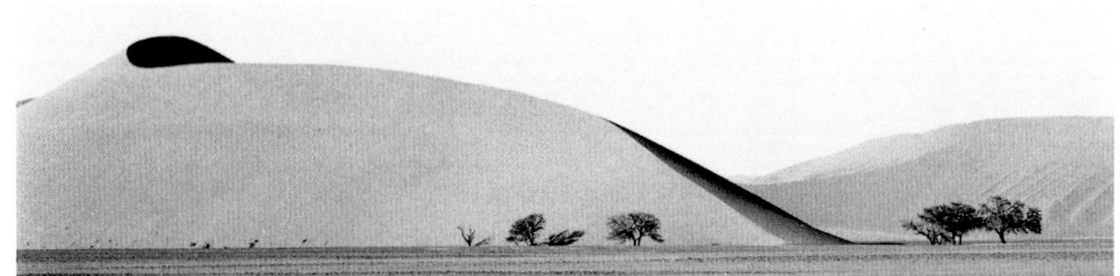

Dune 45, A.M.

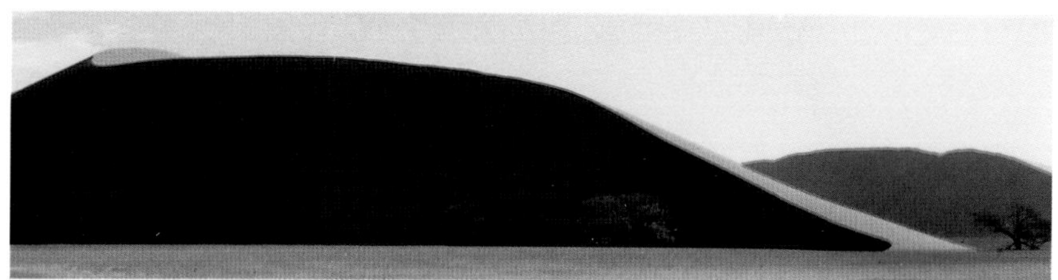

Dune 45, P.M.

Dead pan

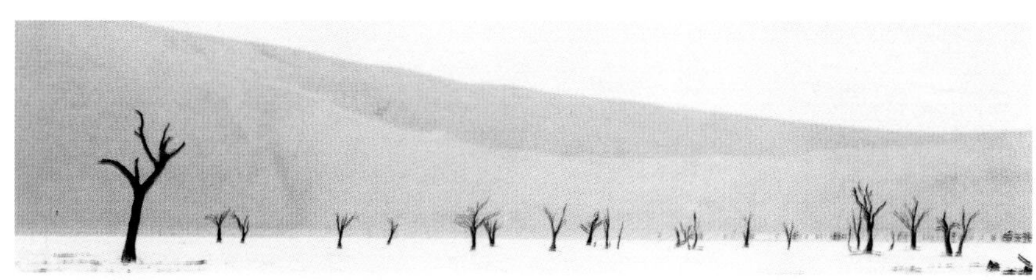

Quivertree in disorder

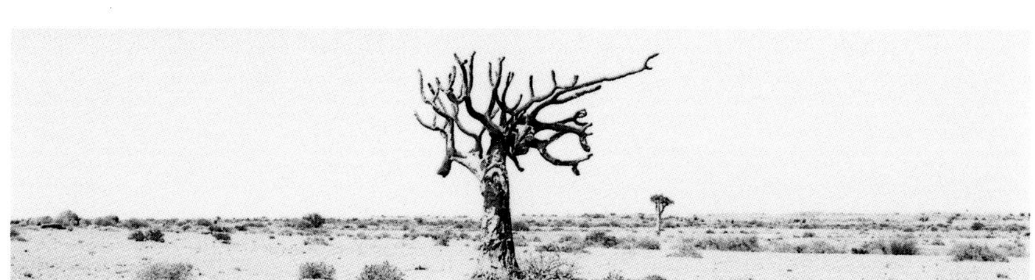

Place of the !Kung

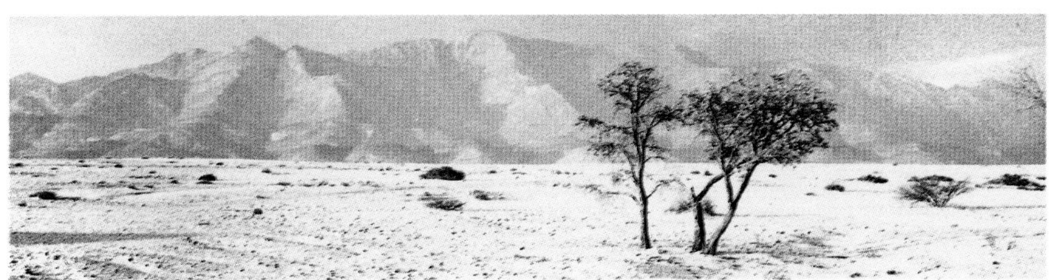

Dead camelthorn

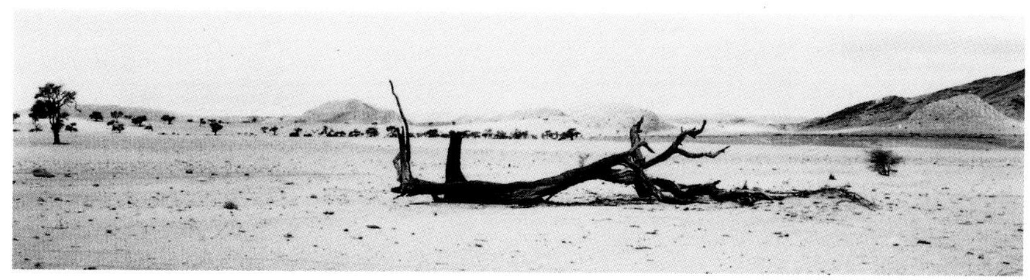

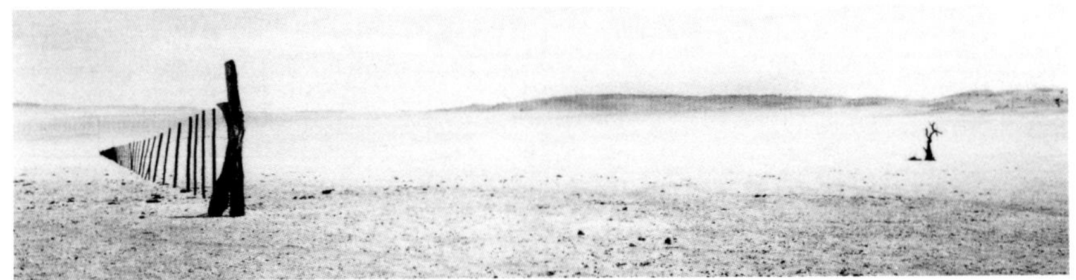

Gatepost to the western pump

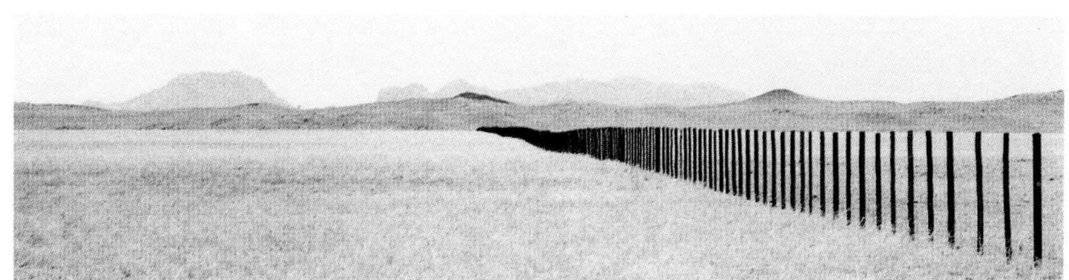

Foot-and-mouth fence

Red snake

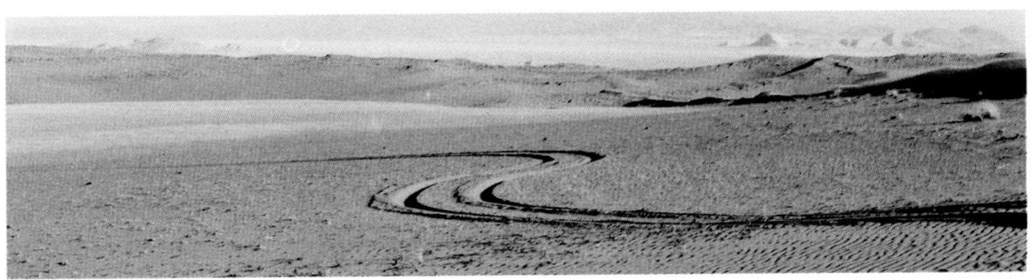

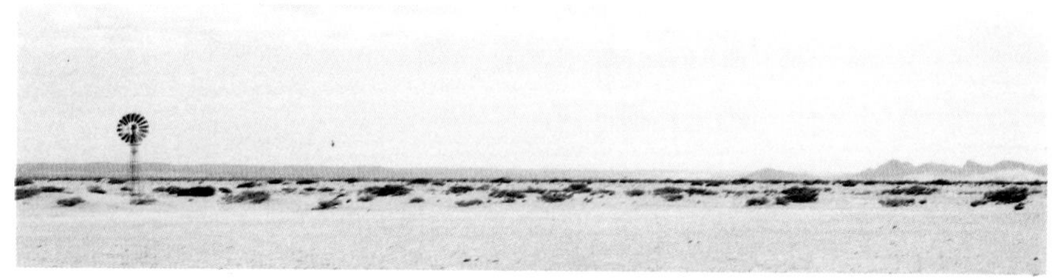

Water!

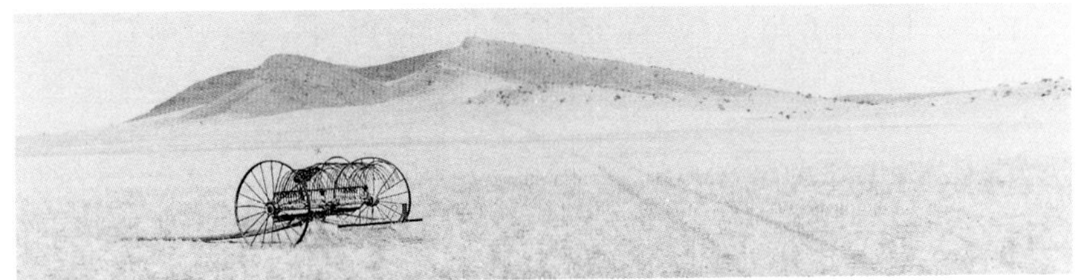

Tsondab Valley farm

Shelter from the wind

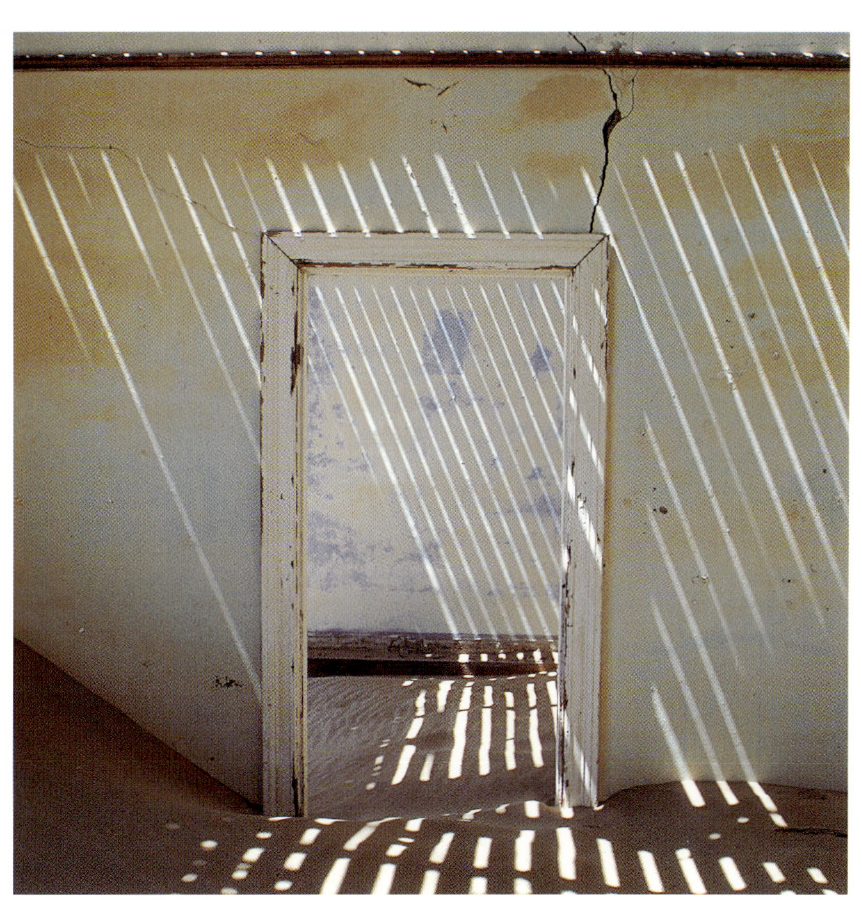

Long road to Solitaire

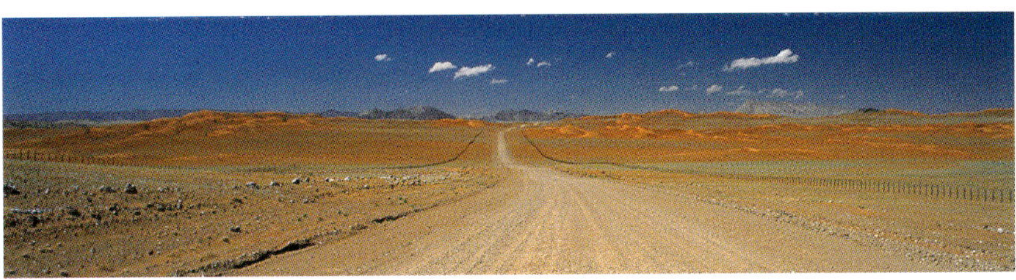

Forgotten village

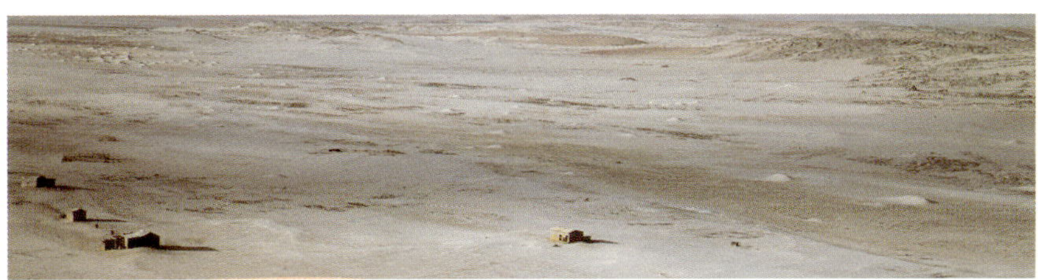

Hangman's tree

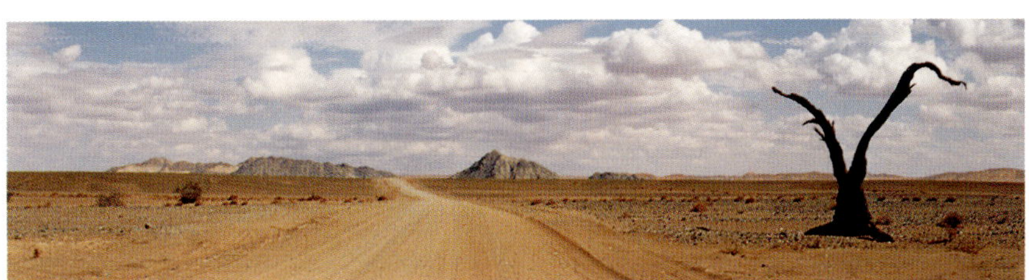

After the rains

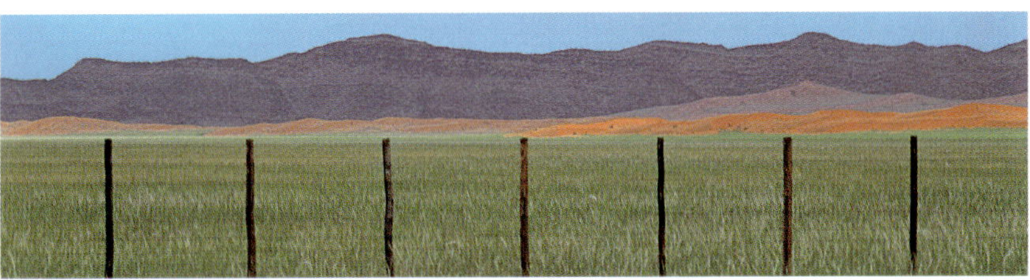

Christmas at Tsondab

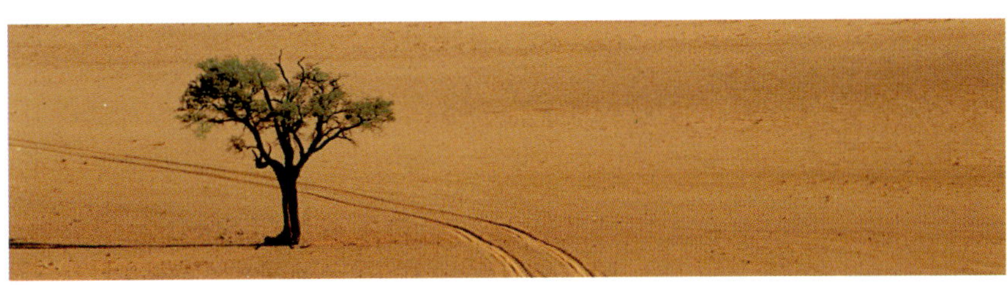

Waiting for rain

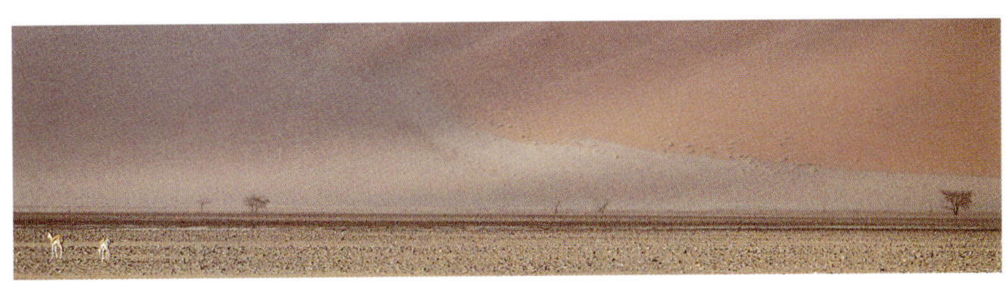

Transhumance

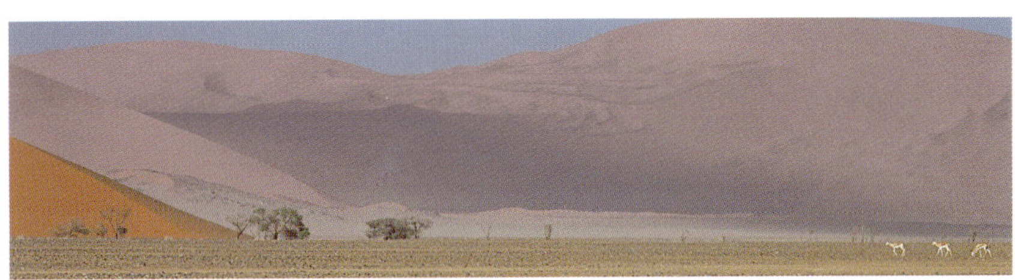

African canvas

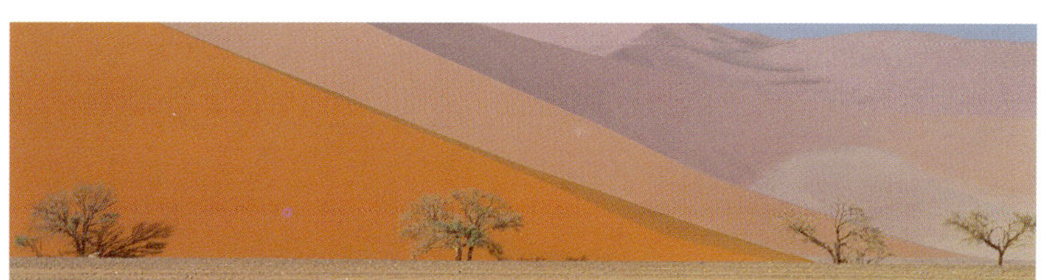

Dead pan before a storm

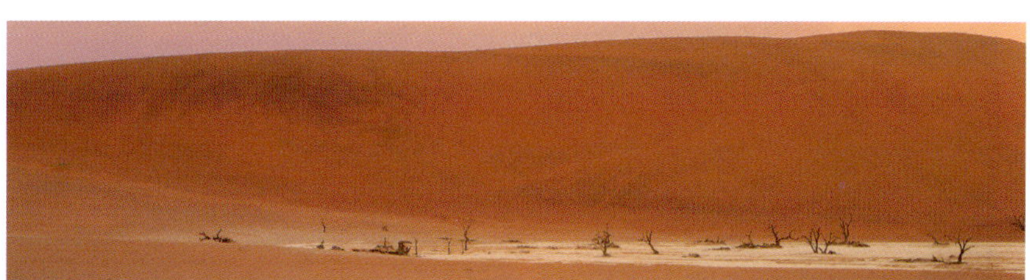

Moonrise over Tsauchab River

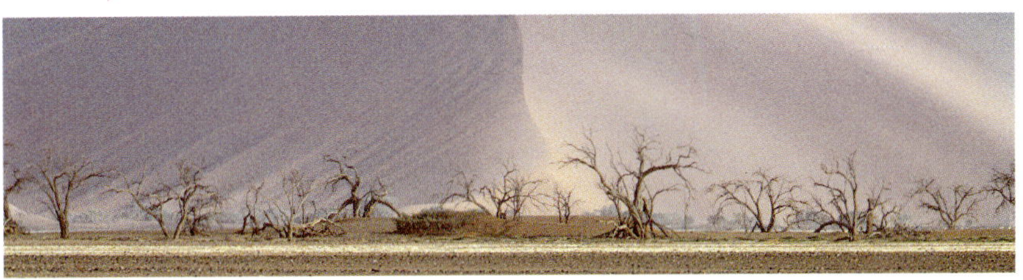

!N'gani's place

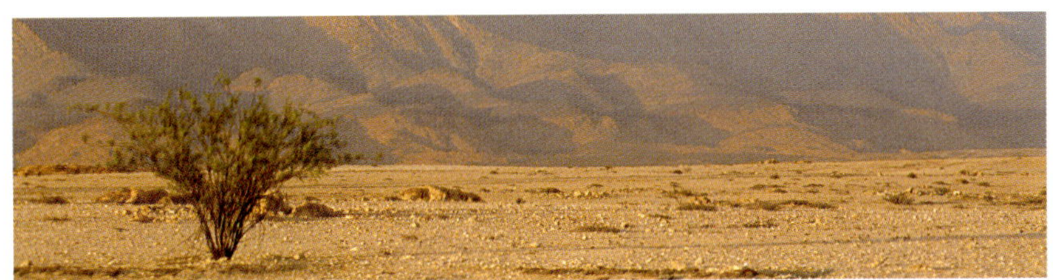

Rebirth

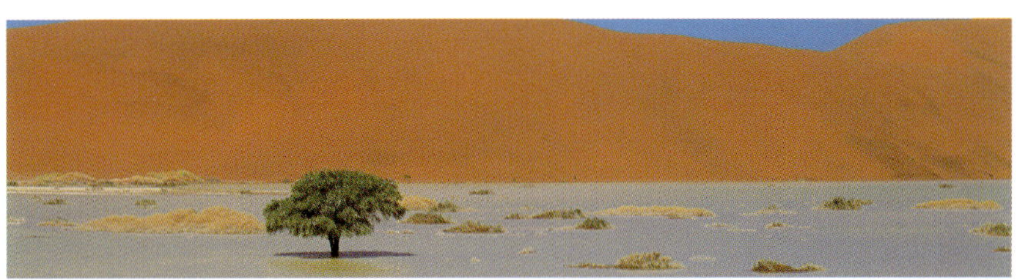

Promise of rain

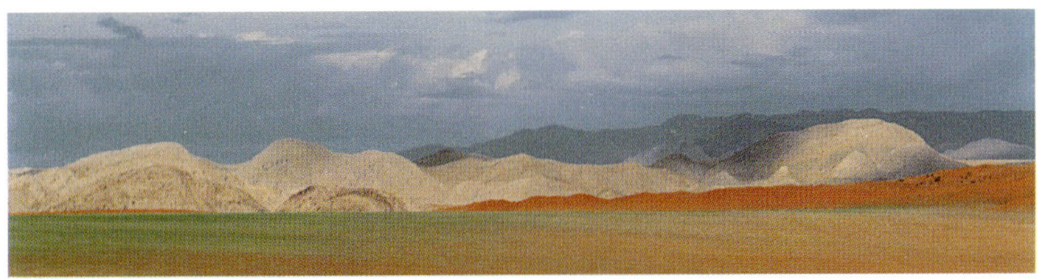

Sisyphus of Erongo

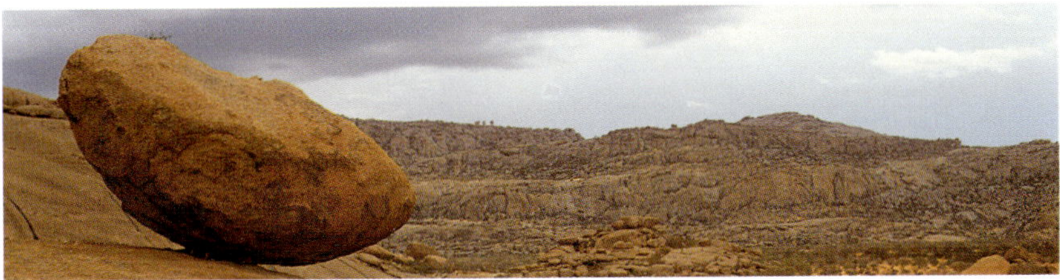

Bushman's Paradise

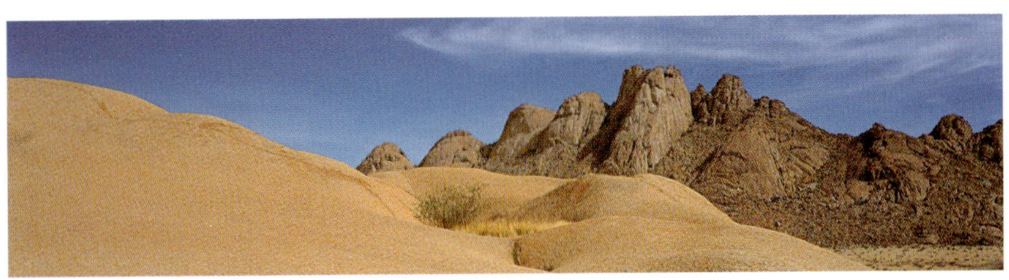

Lost world

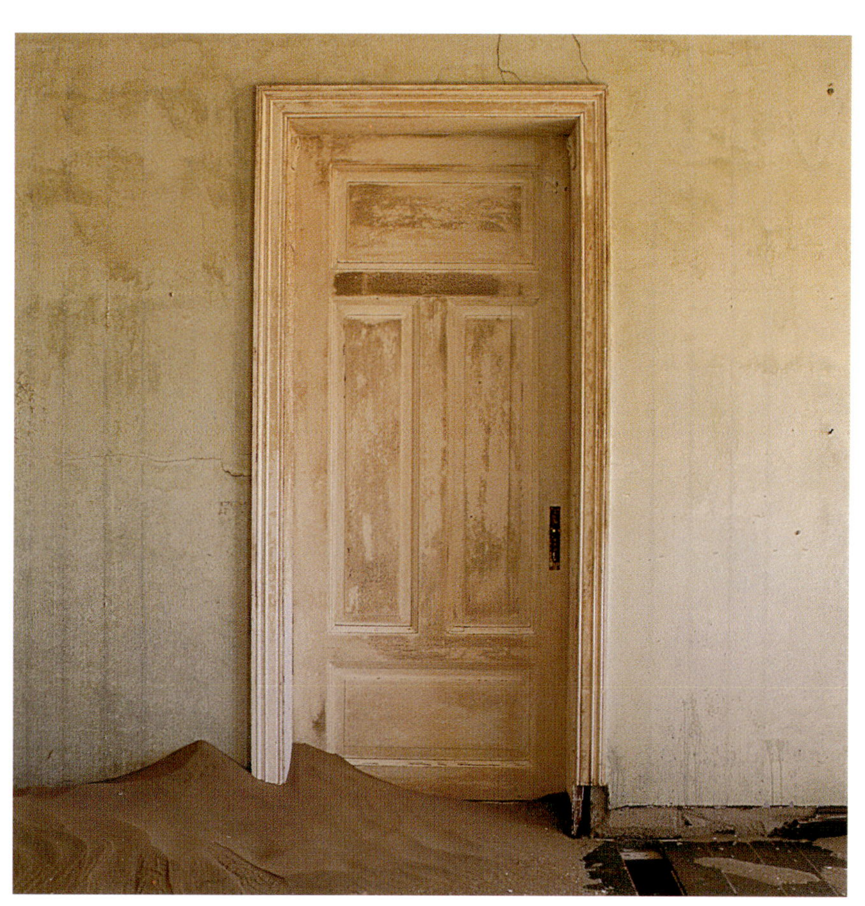

First published in the United States of America in 1997 by
The Monacelli Press, Inc.
10 East 92nd Street, New York, New York 10128.

Library of Congress Cataloging-in-Publication Data
Courtney-Clarke, Margaret, date.
Places in the sand / Margaret Courtney-Clarke.
p.   cm.
ISBN 1-885254-76-8
1. Landscape photography—Namibia. 2. Namib Desert (Namibia)—Pictorial works. I. Title.
TR660.5.C68   1997
779'.366881—dc21   97-28067

Printed and bound in Italy

Designed by Ink, Inc.